THE WATER INSIDE
THE WATER

He goes from death to death, who sees the many here.

—THE VEDANTA

THE WATER
INSIDE
THE WATER

Susan Mitchell

WESLEYAN
UNIVERSITY PRESS
Middletown, Connecticut

ACKNOWLEDGMENTS:

I am grateful to the National Endowment for the Arts for a grant that enabled me to complete this book. I would also like to thank the Fine Arts Work Center in Provincetown and the Artists Foundation in Boston for their support. Grateful acknowledgment is also made to the University of Virginia for a Hoyns Fellowship in Creative Writing and to the MacDowell Colony for a Bernadine Kielty Scherman Fellowship.

Original publication of poems in this book: *The Albemarle Magazine,* "This Morning"; *The American Poetry Review,* "Blackbirds" and "The Trowel"; *The Agni Review,* "The Mouse and the Clock"; *Ironwood,* "Bread" and "The Explosion"; *Kayak,* "The Road" and "Song of Baal"; *The Little Magazine,* "The Promise"; *Shankpainter,* "The Beach at St. Anne's," "The Bear," "Meditations on a Photograph," "The Road Back" under the title "Light and Water," and "Tent Caterpillars."

The Nation first published "Aubade," "The Death" under the title "When Grandfather Died," "Maps," "Once, Driving West of Billings, Montana," and "The Yard Geese."

"Elegy for a Child's Shadow," "From the Journals of the Frog Prince," "Night Tree," and "The Visit" appeared originally in *The New Yorker.*

"From the Journals of the Frog Prince" has been reprinted in *The Norton Introduction to Literature,* edited by Carl E. Bain, Jerome Beaty, and J. Paul Hunter, published by W. W. Norton & Company, third edition, 1981, and in *Getting From Here to There: Writing and Reading Poetry,* by Florence Grossman, published by Boynton Cook Publishers, Inc., 1982.

All inquiries and permissions requests should be addressed to the Publisher, Wesleyan University Press, 110 Mt. Vernon Street, Middletown, Connecticut 06457

Distributed by Harper & Row Publishers, Keystone Industrial Park, Scranton, Pennsylvania 18512

LIBRARY OF CONGRESS CATALOGING IN PUBLICATION DATA

Mitchell, Susan, 1944–
  The water inside the water.

  (Wesleyan new poets)
  I. Title. II. Series.
PS3563.I824W3 1983 811'.54 83-10503
ISBN 0-8195-2110-8
ISBN 0-8195-1114-5 (pbk.)

Manufactured in the United States of America
First Edition

For Robert and Juliet

CONTENTS

I

ONCE, DRIVING WEST OF BILLINGS, MONTANA,

I ran into the afterlife.
No fluffy white clouds. Not even stars. Only sky
dark as the inside of a movie theater
at three in the afternoon and getting bigger all the time,
expanding at terrific speed
over the car which was disappearing,
flattening out empty
as the fields on either side.

                                               It was impossible to think
under that rain louder than engines.
I turned off the radio to listen, let my head
fill up until every bone
was vibrating—sky.

                                     Twice, trees of lightning
broke out of the asphalt. I could smell
the highway burning. Long after, saw blue smoke twirling
behind the eyeballs, lariats
doing fancy rope tricks, jerking silver
dollars out of the air, along with billiard cues, ninepins.

I was starting to feel I could drive forever
when suddenly one of those trees was right in front of me.
Of course, I hit it—
branches shooting stars down the windshield,
poor car shaking like a dazed cow.
I thought this time for sure I was dead
so whatever was on the other side had to be eternity.

Saw sky enormous as nowhere. Kept on driving.

THE ROAD

We are the dust that rises and
settles and rises again.
— SHABAKA

In the car's dream the road offered itself.
That is why we lay down and pressed
our faces into the white line. In the car's dream
the road had just been paved and smelled of tar and paint.
On either side fields sank out of sight
under the weight of the moon
which was full and white and blinded us
so that we had to look away
and into each other's eyes.
That was the moment the road entered us,
winding and unwinding
down the center of our lives.

In the car's dream the road goes on forever.
We kneel by it, we undress
down to the light the moon leaves on our skin.
Then we lie down, our backs flush with the white line,
we stretch out our arms and feel
the road rolling under us, the hills lifting us up.

The road cannot be resisted.
It forces us down
into the ruts, the holes where rain gathers.
Now we know how hungry we always were,
as we fill ourselves with pebbles, with tar and asphalt.
We leave nothing of it.
The white line throbs behind our eyes.
But the road is merciless and forces us on
until our mouths taste of concrete
until our faces are smeared with oil and gasoline.

In the car's dream the road goes on forever.

FOR A FRIEND EATING AN APPLE

There is nothing I want more
than to watch you eat another apple. So please,
start from the beginning and rub a McIntosh or a Granny Smith
on your sleeve to work up a good shine.
Then, bite into it.
When I hear the first crunch of desire,
my mouth flows with the names of apples. But when I watch
you bite through the skin, my mouth fills with fruit.
Now that I have seen you eat an apple,
there can never be enough apples in the world to satisfy me.
Even if I were to buy bushels of them,
brown paper bags spilling over
with green and red and yellow apples,
there would not be enough.
Now that I have watched you eat an apple
my hand is lonely unless an apple fills it.
Only an apple appreciates what it means to have teeth.
Only an apple understands
how teeth want something to resist them,
though not too much,
how teeth want to make an impression,
then take back the impression they have made,
how teeth really don't want blood,
but only a good fight,
how teeth will go on eating and eating
through an entire lifetime
only to satisfy their secret desire
which is to find something they cannot bite through,
something like a core
they have to spit out,
just so the whole process can start over again.

THE YARD GEESE

In my aunt's yard
the geese grew thick as bushes. Each spring
they flapped up white
beside the hydrangeas and hawthorne.
Where the yard sank under puddles
they snapped at grass and old clothesline. Or sniffed the air.
Miles away salt marsh croaked and honked.
Webbed feet broke the water surface.

Mixed with the familiar yard smells,
with car fumes and fresh coffee and incurable damp,
was a new smell—alien, enormous.

All along the eastern Chesapeake geese were splashing down.
Under feather stubs the yard geese felt it—the river.
Behind their eyes they saw it. It shook like blood.
Deep in goose bone, cattails shivered and broke.
The yard geese spread pinioned wings.
They ran. They lifted. They fell back.

Deep in my thigh flesh
goose teeth sank down and refused to let go.
Saliva hissed in my throat.

Cuffing his head and wings
my uncle pulled the gander off me—
the big one who always took corn from my hand
so delicately
his bill had no more weight than a leaf.

In the kitchen my aunt boiled water.
The soap shone red.
The doctor who sewed me up
put in seventeen stitches straight as a picket fence.

Outside, the gander with great precision
leaned sideways
to nip a blade of grass,
then shuffled off on rhubarb legs.

THE BEAR

Tonight the bear
comes to the orchard and, balancing
on her hind legs, dances under the apple trees,
hanging onto their boughs,
dragging their branches down to earth.
Look again. It is not the bear
but some afterimage of her
like the car I once saw in the driveway
after the last guest had gone.
Snow pulls the apple boughs to the ground.
Whatever moves in the orchard—
heavy, lumbering—is clear as wind.

The bear is long gone.
Drunk on apples,
she banged over the trash cans that fall night,
then skidded downstream. By now
she must be logged in for the winter.
Unless she is choosy.
I imagine her as very choosy,
sniffing at the huge logs, pawing them, trying
each one on for size,
but always coming out again.

Until tonight.
Tonight sap freezes under her skin.
Her breath leaves white apples in the air.
As she walks she dozes,
listening to the sound of axes chopping wood.
Somewhere she can never catch up to
trees are falling. Chips pile up like snow.
When she does find it finally,
the log draws her in as easily as a forest,
and for a while she continues to see,
just ahead of her, the moon
trapped like a salmon in the ice.

MAPS

for my father

Don't doubt it, they remember—
the familiar waters passing under them,
your house and you
in the yard, shouting back.

The morning of their return
wasn't I always up before dawn, goose honk
ready to break from my throat
as we watched the ruts filling with their bright rain?

You taught me the paths they leave
in the sky, showed me
the furrows left season after season by wings
coming back. On the palm of my hand
you traced their rivers, the creeks they follow,
pounding into my pulse
the air throb
the wing beat.

What map is there for a man's silence?
For the image sunk like a bullet in his skull, for
the one thing he will never tell you,
which, of course, is the one thing you most want to know?

You taught me the gun, as your father
taught it to you. You fitted
the stock to my shoulder. When you told me to fire,
I felt the bullet moving in
two directions, like love, and when I held the bird up,
there was still a thin strip of sky
in the one eye closing.

PILGRIM HEIGHTS

Do not begin with the spring where supposedly
they knelt and pressed their mouths into sandy
soil for their first drink of American water.
Hold off a while, as they did. Five days
into the New World, they were still drinking
what they'd brought with them,
water that by this time stank of seasickness,
their fevers. Surrounded by sweet water,
they hesitated. Even when only the dregs
remained in the casks, they imagined
the drops elongated, stretched into icicles
they could chew slowly or lick at
through the long winter.

                                  Open your mouth.
I will pour into it the names of ponds,
the ponds of Cape Cod:
Newcomb's, Swett's, Slough, Horse-Leech and Round.
On warm nights in March you can hear the ice
breaking up, the iron bells of Slough
melting into your sleep. The water of Round Pond
is green and tastes like tart apples. The grass
of Horse-Leech whistles as you wade through it.
Sometimes toward sunset a young girl dances
over the ice at Swett's. If she's
wearing red shoes, she may be the Witch
of Billingsgate. No matter how much you want
to glide over the ice with her, stay back
as you would from brackish water. But some
hot afternoon, as you walk through the dunes
near Pilgrim Heights, put your head to the sand.
Listen for the slow drip of water, the melt
of the ancient glacier that scoured out
Cape Cod Bay. Directly under your feet is ice
colder than any you ran your tongue over
as a child, ice so pure you feel invisible

skating it. Listen for its tides,
the lunar tug of its vast moraine where
the dead are skating, the bones of their feet
sharpened by centuries of ice,
William Bradford skating with Miles Standish,
the dried corn they stole from the Indians,
spilling now from their open mouths.

                                          If,
some night, drunk, you lose your way
in those circles dune grass turns,
blowing round and round in the wind,
you may feel the sand shifting
under you as if an hourglass had just broken.
What tastes gritty in your mouth is time. What
blows past you by the fistful is also time.
Lean into it as if you were looking out
over the deck of a ship. Unsteady as you are,
lean further until you no longer resist its pull
and have to fish yourself out, still
shivering with its possibilities.

When you come to, morning flows
amber with needles of pine and juniper,
and hung over though you are,
you find, by sheerest accident, the curve
of a river where an egret, dune-white
flaps up. Accept this blessing,
feel it sweeten your mouth like water
bubbling up from a spring where you drank
as a child, your body golden inside
the tall grass closing over you.

THE DEAD

At night the dead come down to the river to drink.
They unburden themselves of their fears,
their worries for us. They take out the old photographs.
They pat the lines in our hands and tell our futures,
which are cracked and yellow.
Some dead find their way to our houses.
They go up to the attics.
They read the letters they sent us, insatiable
for signs of their love.
They tell each other stories.
They make so much noise
they wake us
as they did when we were children and they stayed up
drinking all night in the kitchen.

THE EXPLOSION

No one is crying.
In fact, there isn't a sound, as if on this street
it has been snowing for years, muffling
the noises of three men and one woman
staring out of the factory window.
That is why it is so hard to find the children.
With so much silence, how could you hear
a child exploding?
The fathers, though, are easy enough to locate.
Theirs are the arms reaching in
from another world.
The children, when they find them, are absolutely white.
In another world they might be made of snow.
You think if a father brushed away the ashes
from his child's face,
he would remember.
The father knows better.
He knows if you saw his child in a dream
you would run away.
The miracle is its almost human form,
the arms spread wide like a snow angel's,
the pencil-thin legs sharpened to points so fine
you cannot see what they are writing on the pavement.
The miracle is the child hasn't blown away yet.
The child does this for the father.
That is why the father is fighting the other men
to get at it. He points to the single shoe as proof.
The others know he is lying.
They know his child has vanished into the pavement.
His child is only that outline drawn hastily
with white chalk.

THE BEACH AT ST. ANNE'S

i

On visitors' afternoons the old men and women,
the grandfathers and grandmothers,
the brothers and sisters, are wheeled outside.
Two sometimes three rows of them,
blankets over their knees, scarves holding up their heads.
The nurses wheel them past a shock of red maples
to a hill near the sea. They look down
on the endless water which never stops
pushing forward and pulling back. My grandmother
keeps on her lap the maple leaves
I have gathered for her. When she puts her hands
over her ears, I say Yes, the sea is noisy.
And when she puts two fingers into her mouth,
digging under her tongue, I do not resist
the shining string of saliva she winds around my finger.
I put the maple leaves into her hands,
I take her hands between mine and rub them.
I rub the sun into them. And the wind.

ii

The path down to the beach is narrow and brilliant white.
This Sunday afternoon the sea is blowing
back on itself, blue scale over blue scale.
I listen to the clouds gathering in the sky.
I listen to my feet kicking up sand.
Against tide, against wind, three gulls rise
and fall with the waves, drifting toward shore.
I listen to their white heads, their white wings.
I listen until I have to ask the world a favor.
I listen until I have to ask
the world to do this one thing for me.
Because even now I am forgetting, I ask
not to forget. I ask that my hands should not forget.
I ask that my feet should not forget.
Because even now I am forgetting
I ask to stay awake forever
only so that I should not forget
those who are forgetting me
those who are forgetting me and asking to be forgotten.

THE ROAD BACK

i

I am coming back,
taking the road I always take
when I come back,
each time through sumac
the half-moons of blown-out tires
the orange berry light.

Everything is as I left it.
But nothing is the same.

When I get to the wagon
the pine planks have weathered.
My thumb breaks through
the rotten wood and the wood motes
shine in the slow light.

ii

The season is indeterminate,
neither fall nor spring, and so is the hour,
nightfall or just before morning.
I always expect you to be there.
The bread tastes different.
The light falls more softly.

Once you rowed me across the lake
in the white boat, my hand trailing water.
Mists were lifting. Neither light nor air, we
headed for a flock of ducks,
rocking with them,
until they flapped up all at once.

I returned scraped and planed
with nor more superfluity
than a drop of water, or a shadow.

iii

This is all the reverence I can summon,
to stand before water,
before the depth of the world,
reflected or drowned,
ponds, rivers, lakes,
where my face falls and breaks
like a stone.

I remember the tall grass,
knotting and unknotting itself
in the rain, though
I am not sure
what I heard was the grass
or the rain.

iv

Sometimes I jump from memory to memory
as if I were running
along stones in a stream.
More often, I don't get farther
than the wagon
which may not be a wagon, after all,
but a box coming apart
in a field, the pine boards
split by ice
or gnawed, the light
opening the knotholes.

Sometimes I suspect your face
is fully light
or a darkness so pure I can see
myself in it
where I kneel and rise,
broken endlessly and blessed.

ELEGY FOR A CHILD'S SHADOW

Perhaps the moment included a bench, a tree with a bicycle
leaning against it, and a shadow.
From the position of the shadow, the mother
might know whether something
was entering, or just leaving. And whether,
if it was leaving, it would be back.

                                 If she had to describe
the shadow, she would say it is shaped like a sundial
in a park where all afternoon children have been playing.
Or she would say it is like a pool
where golden fish swim. When the sun is at a certain angle,
she can hear the water inside the water,
and what she thinks of is a life
dissolving slowly
like a wafer in the mouth of a child.

The fish swim in the pool without expectations.
She feeds them leaves and grass,
but they refuse to eat. Perhaps they feed on time.
Is it necessary to know whether leaves
which have been falling into the pool all afternoon
are floating face up or face down? Or whether
the fish are able to see through clouds
reflected in the water?

                           Sometimes death is humble,
merely a space
tempting a child to fill it with itself.
As the grass, so plush and blue,
tempts the mother. Lying there, she hears
the sound of rain exciting the leaves
to stillness, and later,
much later, she feels the dark
gliding gently as an eraser over her life.

THE VISIT

This time I will set the table, I will place
the woman before the bread she is about to cut.
I will tell the man carrying in the basket of peaches
to shout from the door. I will nod
to the man pouring wine and he will begin to cough.

Chairs will scrape against the kitchen floor.
Autumn light will glaze the long board that is the table.
One woman will begin to slice the cheese,
a big cheese yellow as buttercups.

At this point it is my turn to walk through the door.
I am ten or twelve. I don't know anyone in the room.
Someone will cut bread for me.
My glass will drip wine. And when I leave
walking between father and mother
one man will give me an apple.

Mother will smile, father will close the trunk of the car.
Someone will come running with peaches.
The sun will be red as wine on the grass.
Sealing the horizon will be a thin strip of gold.
Just as I bite into the apple—
a red apple with one fleck
yellow as the thin strip of horizon—
a pheasant will start across the road.

A PROMISE

My grandmother said I would have
blue-black hair, hair
black and shiny as the feathers of a crow
or the ebony keys of a piano.

It didn't work out as she hoped.
My hair is brown.

Sometimes I wonder who
she was thinking of when she prayed
over my hair.
Was it the heroine of a Russian novel,
all her thick blackness wound
high and back to show off
her broad forehead, her white skin?

But my grandmother didn't read.
So she must have had someone else in mind,
someone she loved so much
she wanted to see
his hair growing out of me.

When my father was young
his hair was black
as trees caught in the rain.
In bright sunlight
bits of blue and purple
hit my eyes like
a peacock's tail suddenly
exploding.
I thought hair that color
could never change.

MEDITATIONS ON A PHOTOGRAPH

"When you look at me that way
you look just like my mother. . . ."

This said by my own mother.
But in this last photo taken of my grandmother
she looks like someone we'd never known,
as if at the last moment
she's realized another possibility and become it
without warning or the least hesitation.
Whenever mother looks at the picture she says
"You can see she is dying there."
Can you? Can you see it?
The picture was taken August 23, 1965
at my aunt's beach house overlooking Conscience Bay.
The time is a little after lunch,
a long lunch that must have gone on until two or three.
Some of what we were eating is in the photo—
bread, ham and a bunch of green grapes.
Grandmother should have been sitting between
me and two of her daughters. But at the last moment
she leaned forward, reaching out of the picture,
as if she wanted to stop the photographer
or had something urgent to say.
She blurred part of the photo. The leaves are smeared.
I could be looking at them through a rain-streaked window.
And for whatever eternity a photo has
there will be a silver streak
where she elbowed a knife off the table.

"Look at the eyes." That's mother again.
One of grandmother's eyes is rheumy, enflamed,
the eye of an old and decrepit bird,
a maddened eye,
fixed, staring out at the world, angry
at what it can no longer see.
I follow it back
into the skull, pulled inward, sucked
into the brain where the anger burns aimlessly,
a blind hole
beyond the reaches of us whose eyes
swing lightly over trees, houses, hands and other eyes.

Then there's the mouth—smiling, open, working
against the eye, denying the meaning of the eye, insisting
that the eye, like the hand lifting
the grapes, only wants—what? What does it want?
The hand lifts out of the photo, the eye
leads back in. I weave in and out, sometimes
thinking the eye must have been caught unawares,
before it could compose itself
into the weakly tearing eye
Grandmother always wiped with a white handkerchief.

Perhaps the problem with the photo is my expectations.
For example, I've always been surprised
by my pale skin, the almost overexposed cheeks
and the purple shadows deepening
under the eyes, even surrounding my face.
There is something latent about them
as if they had always been just under the skin
waiting for this photo to bring them out
the way air brings out the blue of potatoes.

Or take the grapes. Are they really grapes?
They could be a green skull. See
where some grapes are missing—
you have the eye sockets.
And there, where we must have eaten quite a few,
a gaping hole that could be a mouth.
The longer I look at it
the more clearly I see inside
each grape a tiny skull. . . .

Maybe the picture isn't important.
After all, grandmother didn't choose to be in it.
She hardly touched any of the food.
Her legs hurt her all afternoon. Perhaps
her hand is pointing to what the photographer left out—
the wind, salty and fresh, the buzz
of a seaplane and the beach tilting slightly
upward, where only that morning I had picked mussels.
Grandmother spotted them. The shells,
purple-black under the water, were opening,
the orange tongues sticking out.
We sat on the beach and ate them out of their shells.
Then we watched the wake of a boat.
One wave came in to the shore. The other wave,
lifting like the fin of an enormous fish,
continued out to sea.

TENT CATERPILLARS

for Nathaniel, 1900–1968

All afternoon you worked at cutting them down.
Branch after branch tossed
into the heap. You had your ceremony. Old pants. The pipe.
The pipe rested in the cleft of the tree.
When the pile got big enough, you threw the kerosene.

Now the woods are clouded again. You forgot
the world could be this messy.
Air thickens into leaves, the leaves into worms.
Behind the barn, overnight, it seems,
tents have spread out in the apple trees.

There's work for you. So you come back
in your pants old as dirt. With a pipe heavy as stone.
No time to lose. Whatever is rotten,
whatever won't hold the weight of another season,
you hack down. There's one moment, though,

when you feel almost sorry for them.
The tents break into flame and the small, black
pieces of anguish crawl
out into the grass. Those that get away, well,
you let them get away this time.

THE WINDOW

You lie face down on the bed,
near the edge, so you can look out the window:
brick wall almost close enough to touch,
then someone else's window,
Coke bottle propping it open.

You lie face down, naked, no wind
blowing across your back as you watch the light
moving along the brick wall.
You watch how it fastens there,
scratching with long nails.
Then you notice on the molding
that runs under the ceiling of your room
a roach. It was moving until you looked at it.
Now it hangs there,
expanding/contracting, which is the way,
you decide, roaches breathe.

In another room, which does not exist unless
you bother to remember it, light
buzzes near a window
trying
to get back to the lawn.
You stand at the window watching.
Behind you, a man sleeps on a bed, a woman next to him.
Now you turn and take a good look at your mother and father.
They lie on their backs, mouths open,
practicing what it's like to be dead.

There is really no point in going out.
But you go out.
Light moves along the pavement like chalk
across a blackboard. You do not
want to listen to it. But you listen anyway.
The sound takes a long time.
Ahead of you, a boy in a white T-shirt is making a sound too,
the sound of a tin can being kicked along a street.

THE DEATH

I heard the crying and came closer.
Father was sitting in the half-filled bathtub.
He wasn't covering his face with his hands.
He was crying into the air.
Mother was washing him. She ran the soapy cloth
round and round on his chest.
After a while, he sat on the side of the tub
and she dried him.
Then he took the towel and put it over his face.

I walked out of the house certain I would not come back.
Downstairs a neighbor's daughter was tearing
leaves off a hedge. When we rubbed the leaves into our hands
our hands turned green. I put my green hands
on her face and wondered where I would go
now that I was never coming back.
I walked to the subway station
and for hours I watched the trains going east
to Coney Island. Then I went back.

When mother told me
we were sitting in the car, just the two of us.
I must have climbed
out of the front seat because
I see myself sitting alone in the back
in the not quite dark. I have taken
my father's canvas hat from the floor
and put it on my head. Through its visor
the first green night is coming on.
A green woman is rocking a green carriage.
A green man sits and smokes on his green stoop.

III

SONG OF BAAL

for they were no gods, but the work
of men's hands, wood and stone;
therefore, they were destroyed.
        —II Kings 19:18

You combed my hair.
You pulled lice from my skin.
You bathed my hoofs and made wreaths of flowers
to hang around my neck.
And in my way I loved you.
Each night I rose luminous at your window
and the window opened to let me in.
I pressed my thighs against yours
and you said, Father.
I buried my head in the rich folds of your belly
and you said, Son.
You bit the nipples of my chest and said, Mother.
I was everything to you.
I brought calves to your cows, lambs to your ewes.
You said you were happy.

But one night when I bloomed
outside your window
you spoke of fear.
Hard with love, I grabbed your breasts
and wedged myself inside your skin.
Don't let me die, you said.
Don't let my children die.
I'll give you my little finger.
I'll give you my gold earrings.
Patiently, I endured your ignorance,
your talk of magic stones, elixirs of life, and trees
breathless with immortality.
Doesn't the grass smell sweet? I said.
Have you ever seen a moon like this one, tonight?

A week later you kicked me out.
At first I was angry.
I trampled the corn in the fields, pulled up
the wheat from the earth, crushed
the figs on the trees. I smashed
my own temples, my own shrines, packed off the whores
and sent them back to their fathers.
But finally, I sat in the dust and cried.
Idiot! I called to you, The blood is dumb.
Idiots! You and your children will stand sleepless
in the open fields. Fear will sit on your bed, a rat,
teeth white as the moon.
Each night it will beat at the window and
the window will open to let it in.

THE MOUSE AND THE CLOCK

It has just started to snow,
one large flake on the red roof of the house,
two small flakes on the black cap of a boy.
In the light of the street lamp flakes circle like moths.
Inside the house a woman sits in a chair
and behind her, like a mother reading over her shoulder,
is a tall, thin clock with a white face and gold hands.
Tick-tock, tick-tock, it says
like a tongue flicking in and out.
Tock-tick, you must read to the beat of my heart.
And slowly the story the woman is reading
shapes itself to the beat of the clock.
Tock-tock, says the clock to the child in the next room,
You must dream to the beat of my heart.
But the child, who is not asleep yet,
sits up when it hears the clock speak.
Look! says the child. *It's snowing.*
The snow must fall to the beat of my heart, says the clock.
And the wind must wind and unwind to my key.
The moon, too, it must rise and set to my chimes.
But the snow isn't listening.
And the story the snow has to tell
rises and falls, loosens and tightens
to a rhythm only the snow knows.

The woman puts down her book
saying, *This story is not very good,*
when she hears a voice
smaller than the hole in a button,
finer than the point of a needle.
I, says the voice, *am a mouse.*
And this is true, for a mouse
has come out of the oven and now it sits
in the center of the room.
Its ears are red, its tail is red
and skinny like the leather marker in her book.
The mouse looks at her with its tiny red eyes.
Then it begins to dance, shouting:
Chalk for the nose, hair for the bag.
Nasty the whisker and worse the tail.
Tick-tock, tick-tock, says the clock. *That's nonsense!*
But as the mouse speaks its voice grows bigger
until it is big as the buckle on the woman's belt,
and bigger until it is big as the shoe on her foot,
until it is big as the voice of the child
calling from the next room.
Look! says the voice. *It's snowing.*
And for the first time that evening she looks at the snow.
When she does, the snow is so loud that for a moment
she cannot hear the clock speaking.
Tick-tock, says the clock. But she really cannot hear it.
Instead she hears the moon.
And it seems to her that the moon
is a clock without hands and without numbers.
One, says the moon, *One.*
Two, says the moon, *Two.*
Listen, says the child, *the moon is chiming.*

THIS MORNING

On a morning like this, clean and blue and shining,
I remember I am earth,
my hair has a long way to grow.
I am walking to the bay.
There is no one to see I am alone, I am happy, I am naked.
The blackberries are ripe. Their seeds stick between my teeth.
Who do I have to forget all this?
Everything is opening—
the hollow of a tree pours honey,
a rabbit holds me with its orange eyes.

FROM THE JOURNALS OF THE
FROG PRINCE

In March I dreamed of mud
sheets of mud over the ballroom chairs and table
rainbow slicks of mud under the throne.
In April I saw mud of clouds and mud of sun.
Now in May I find excuses to linger in the kitchen
for wafts of silt and ale
cinnamon and riverbottom
tender scallion and sour underlog.

At night I cannot sleep.
I am listening for the dribble of mud
climbing the stairs to our bedroom
as if a child in a wet bathing suit ran
up and down them in the dark.

Last night I said: Face it you're bored!
How many times can you live over with the same excitement
that moment when the princess leans
into the well her face a petal
falling to the surface of the water
as you rise like a bubble to her lips
the golden ball bursting from your mouth?
To test myself I said
remember how she hurled you against the wall
your body cracking open
skin shriveling to the bone
your small green heart splitting like a pod
and her face imprinted with every moment
of your transformation?

I no longer tremble.

Night after night I lie beside her.
"Why is your forehead so cool and damp?" she asks.
Her breasts are soft and dry as flour.
The hand that brushes my head is feverish.
At her touch I long for wet leaves
the slap of water against rocks.

"What are you thinking of?" she asks.
How can I tell her
I am thinking of the green skin
shoved like wet pants behind the Directoire desk?
Or tell her I am mortgaged to the hilt
of my sword, to the leek green tip of my soul?
Someday I will drag her by her hair
to the river—and what? Drown her?
Show her the green flame of my self rising at her feet?
But there's no more violence in her
than in a fence or a gate.

"What are thinking of?" she whispers.
I am staring into the garden.
I am watching the moon
wind its trail of golden slime around the oak,
over the stone basin of the fountain.
How can I tell her
I am thinking that transformations are not forever?

IV

LETTERS TO A HOSPITAL

i

In the first dream of the night,
which is also the last
since it wakes me and I get up and sit near the window,

I look out at the trains rolling by
your hospital room. As each train passes
I write down its number,
I lie down on your bed and wait
for the numbers to repeat.

You have gone to a concert
with the other patients, your skin
bandaged to your bones, your bones tied
to your breath. That way you sing better.
I hear you singing
above the oboes and clarinets.
What you sing is so different
the trains stop for a moment to listen.

I turn my face to the wall.
Yours stares through
from the other side, pouring into the room
like a searchlight, the brakes
jam in your throat.
You are saying my name over and over,
which is the punishment here
for singing
against the music.

I write down the number of the song.

ii

I am this emptiness near the window.
I am this place where nobody
sits day after day
watching a river.
My name is God.
My name is Mother.
My name is whatever you love most.

The river is deep as morphine.
It fills my lap.
You can watch the lights of lovers
rocking me. Rain
streams down the window.

Through the rain
you can see another river.
Rats swim there, all night they look
at the moon
which is the last tooth
in the sky.

You can call my name, if you like.
I won't go away.
I'm here for the duration.
I'm here to stay.

iii

After every visit, I'm a little smaller.
Soon I'll be small
as a fetus. Holding me up to the light,
you'll shake out my name,
and thinking it's time to be born,
I'll stir
in my formalin bath.
I'll have my first bad dream.

The fetus
father kept in the library—
unbearably white, it looked at me
through closed lids. It needed someone
to love it, maybe. I pulled it out
by its broken stem. I held it tight and rocked it.
Six months old for fifty years,
it was still waiting for its mother.
Even when its shadows started to flake
in my hands, I rocked it.

           iv

I did something I shouldn't have done.
That's why you're here.
It doesn't matter that I was a child.
I did this thing.
Now you're coal falling down a chute.

Something burns inside my head.
The dead are eating the living.
The living are eating the dead.
What does it matter?
I did something I shouldn't have done.
On a night so beautiful
I hope I never forget it.

Our mother went weeping down the sky.
Now the moon is grafted
to your knees.

Each night I take out your picture.
The pain is so old
it crumbles when I touch your face.
I blow it off my fingers.
At communion I bite into your tears.
You slap me.
That is grace.

V

For your birthday
I bought you a fish in a glass bowl.
All day it leaned its head
against the water, breathing enormously.

During dinner, it glowed like a candle.
When you were ready for bed,
it lit up like a clock, ticking
into the farthest reaches of your sleep.

*

You grew sick of it. I brought it home.
Tonight I woke to hear it
flopping on the floor, and found it
wrapped in Kleenex under the bed.

As if darkness was all
the container it wanted now, it leaped again.
Once back in water,
it dashed itself against the bowl

for hours, until the water opened
like a gill. Excitement
stuck its bone in my throat.
The fish shot up like breath.

I ran a thumb along its neck,
at first to calm it.
The thumb bent back. I grabbed
the fish with both my hands.

And heard its darkness crack.

vi

Listen, I don't need to sleep anymore.
I don't need to wash either.

Just before morning the boats
float like clouds above the river, and lopsided,
misshapen as the head of a newborn
child, the last dream
of the night begins. Slick as oil, it circles
over the lost oars, the rusted springs of a car.
Half perfume, half stench, its amber
regurgitation washes up
into the sleep of gulls, sending them
screaming into the air.

I used to think the dream spread from gull
to gull like a fever.
Now I believe it's the dream
of an entire species, a single wave
breaking over every gull at the same moment.

If I were a lighthouse keeper,
this is when I would turn toward shore.
I would shine into every room in the hospital.
I would pull the river up
to the patients' chins.
I would number their breaths.
I would tell the nurse on night duty to go home.

V

THE MEETING

Tonight above a river nameless
to me the moon is rising
through all the holes in my life, through
floorboards, through the dumb
questions of skull.

A wing lifts inside me,
the broken one, and I breathe in
the will to fall and keep on falling.

A thousand miles to the north
the first flakes of snow rise out of the darkness.
As in a dream I see your house
burst into light,
the only light for miles around,
and you at the table,
head bowed as if listening.

When did you first suspect
you were not coming back
to this body
though its eyes filled
with blood of all the lives
you were leaving?

When I'm numb enough
I'll think I've always been here
waiting for you
to plow the river up,
its deep furrows of silence.

POWDER

Sleep was our first language,
older than milk. When the tongue was backwards,
sleep was the one word we shared.
We said it over and over
until it grew like a cocoon around us.
Each time I was about to waken,
you entered me as snow enters snow. Two moths,
we dozed, swaying
in a numbness of light.

That the leaves were watching made a difference.
Later the moon slid
under my hands
like a banister. The house breathed
louder. From the stove the coals called out for the tree.

Tonight my legs feel slow as wool, Mother. Why
won't you let me sleep? Father sleeps
like a seed inside me. His mouth grows toward my breasts.
Somewhere a house is burning.
Ashes break like moths from the roof.
Who should I rescue? In the attic
your voice hums like a wheel. I lie down on the sled.
Outside, children are skating. They fly by like trees.
Their skates leave clefts of blood in the snow.

BREAD

Slowly the taste of bread rises into my life,
the bread I was given each morning
before I left for school.
Now I reach for the steaming slice,
the loaf I walked on
to keep my shoes shiny and clean.

When a voice tells me to sit down
in the bus with the other fifth graders,
I sit down.
That is the teacher talking.
She is taking us to the place where bread is made.

At night I have dreamed it,
the workers robed in white like nurses,
beads of sweat falling from their foreheads
into enormous vats,
and the teacher warning us
not to fall in. But I know when her back is turned
a child throws itself into a vat,
giving its life to the bread.

When no one is looking, the mothers
mix in their own blood,
the blood a mother hides under one nail
as she lays out her child's clothes,
the little drops you never notice
as she buttons you into your life.

Humbly, I accept the miniature loaf
a woman offers each of us before we leave,
along with a postcard:
a girl holding out a sheaf of wheat tied with red ribbon.
A red kerchief half covers her blond hair.
Her mouth smiles up into mine.

Though I know she's a lie, I keep her
under my pillow.
At night I hear the dull machinery of the wheat
turning through her hair, the squeals
of the mice
as the combine slices into their lives.

Slowly the smell of bread rises
from her hands and with it a draft from the cold room
where someone tries to sleep
before getting up in the dark to go to work
and the T.V. which is smashed one night and the bruise
starting to show on a woman's cheek
as she sweeps up the broken glass,

the bruise inside the man's fist
as he stands over her,
which opens his hand in the morning
and closes it at night,
which he takes from the bread and the bread from the grain,
which can never be thrashed out
no matter how the bread sings like a fly
in a child's hand
no matter how hard the horse kicks
when it is beaten
 no matter how the soil blooms each spring in furrows
of yellow and violet and delicate pink

that dark place under the crust
where the earth
keeps bleeding into my life.

THE STILLBORN

i

If there are still houses
in those shadows,
if there are windows with faces
looking out,
perhaps a child will look in,
calling a name
for the wind to carry away. . . .

At night the family sits down to dinner,
the mother's face gleaming,
the knives and forks
cold as snow in the children's hands.
Once I knocked at the door.
No one remembered me,
my face reshaped by the wind.

ii

Sometimes at night I watch you
walking home across the dark fields.
Shyly, my body offers itself again.
A star comes out, then another,
circling me
with their desires.

iii

I am cutting a blue path through the snow.
At the end of it is a house,
the door blown open.
When I go in,
a woman shadows me with her body.

I am sinking
into a death so warm it
beats like a heart.

In time it may
even call me by name.

DROWNED GIRL

for F. W.

When they found me
the moon was rising through my skin,
my eyes grown larger
from giving off so much light.
Now the lake is frozen over.
Dark birds feed on the snow.
All afternoon I watched
you throw them scraps of bread
until shadows
filled my hands. I wanted to ask,
did they really get to me in time?
But lying there beside you,
I felt the lake's blueness
returning like sleep.

THE STAIRCASE

i

Sometimes before falling asleep I drift
past enormous rooms. Night pours through the windows.
In one room men and women are drinking wine.
They cluster around me.
Moonlight hums at their wrists.
Wine hums in our glasses.
The toasts we make are cruel, each toast
crueler than the one before.
The room gets hotter and hotter, hums
like a high-voltage wire. By now
we are all quite drunk.
What they say to me is unforgivable. I buzz like a flower.
When I awake, my lips are swollen with the sound.

ii

No one should have died. Only the light
should have grown older, ripening on our arms.
When I walk past the old cemetery,
I hear the dead humming in their graves,
the coins on their tongues turning round and round.
After a while, everything hums:
two bones near my throat, the milk in my breasts.
If I press my hand to my belly,
I feel the terrible hush.
I could hold them all
in the palm of my hand and listen.

iii

Once I heard you just ahead of me,
a darkness descending.
I followed through room after room,
the women burning like candles, the men in black tie.
When we came to the room
without windows
you showed me how the body opens.

Sometimes I feel your voice in my mouth.
What it says makes me burn with shame.
I want to bring you back.
I want to heal the earth.
I want to grow wings
and crawl
through the dark on my belly.

The air is a flower.
It opens. Slowly, it takes me in.
I am rising, legs hanging deep into the darkness.
At the center, stars swarm,
humming with the murderous love of the universe.
Then the flower closes.

NIGHT TREE

Walking out late—
the earth white as my breath
and not a car in sight—
I pass a house and in the small
light of the stars
see a man and woman embracing
on their frozen lawn, his
dark leaning over her lesser dark
and the two of them rocking
back and forth, digging in until
they become a tree, swaying
out of the snow.

Sometimes, walking home late, I see
the antlers of a great December stag and
hold to them until they turn
into a branch or a bush, leaving
the world more desolate and bare
than it was before
I thought anything living shared it
with me. And I think to a time
when the loose snow
fluttering against my face
was as much joy
as I could bear for one night.

Such nights are merciful.
Darkness lifts me home and unthinking
the key fits the lock. I find
the bed without turning on a single light
and if I am lucky, I fall asleep
before I have time to think of you.
When I am less fortunate
you sit beside me
on the bare mattress of the soul
or, like tonight, you come to me
familiar as a tree that splits
gradually in two.

THE TROWEL

The trowel a woman left in her garden
takes root and blooms in the rain. Now she listens
to the buds opening against the cellar window.

This sound is not the same as
the sound of the rain. It is more like a slip of the tongue,
saying, "begin" when you meant to say "put an end to."

Tomorrow the woman will look for her trowel.
We should not feel superior
because here in the garden we know things
she cannot possibly know. A new sound

has entered her life, which is different from
the sound of rain beating against a window.
When the woman undresses for bed
she hears it digging under the stairs
and thinks it must be the dog
or else the wind
which lately has learned how to imitate a dog
with a bone in its jaws.

For a moment the woman is terrified
the sound will come weeping into her room
like an arm or leg that's been shut out in the rain
for years. Almost without thinking, she strokes it
with her gardening gloves.
All night it begs forgiveness
for digging up her life.

BLACKBIRDS

Because it is windy, a woman
finds her clothesline bare, and without rancor
unpins the light, folding it into her basket.
The light is still wet. So she irons it.
The iron hisses and hums. It knows how to make the best of things.
The woman's hands smell clean. When she shakes them out,
they are voluminous, white.

All night my hands weep in gratitude
for little things. That feet are not shoes.
That blackbirds are eating the raspberries. That parsley
does not taste like bread.

From now on I want to live
only by grace. In other words, not to deserve things.
Without rancor, the light dives down
among the turnips. I eat it with my stew.

Today the woman's hands smell like roots. When she
shakes them out, they are voluminous, green.
All day they shade me
from the sun. The blackbirds have come to sit in them.
Since this morning, the wind has been enough.

AUBADE

i

When I empty the pitcher
it pours light and the dried body of a moth.
This is how people drown—in light, in air.
With the shadblow white fire over their heads.
They sit down in the woods. We wait
for them to catch their breath. Or, they sit up in bed,
their skin blue as water. And we wait for them to rise.
We hold them as a river holds water.

ii

All spring you tried to flow away.
At night I bound you
to the darkness. I closed the piano
to keep the music in. You tried so hard

to be nothing. The trees flowed out
through their buds. The roots
dreamed they were blossoms, they had learned

how to fly. How much is lost this way?

iii

In the woods light makes a place for itself.
It lies down beside me. It calls me by name.
If I close my eyes,
I find you, a woman in a house by a river.

You hold up a pitcher,
and your voice is blue and heavy as water.
On your hand, a mark like a moth.
When you pour, I am filled with forgetting.

ABOUT THE AUTHOR

A graduate of Wellesley College and Georgetown University, SUSAN MITCHELL is working on her Ph.D. at Columbia University. She has been a Henry Hoyns Fellow at the University of Virginia (1980–81), a fellow at the Fine Arts Center in Provincetown (1977–79), and now teaches at Middlebury College. Mitchell won the Discovery/*The Nation* award poetry contest in 1979 and received a grant from the National Endowment for the Arts in 1981–82. She lives in Middlebury, Vermont.

ABOUT THE BOOK

The text and display type are Bembo. Composition and typesetting were done by Carolinatype of Durham, North Carolina. The book was printed on 60 lb. Warren's Olde Style paper and bound in Holliston Roxite by Kingsport Press, Kingsport, Tennessee. Design and production were by Joyce Kachergis Book Design & Production, Bynum, North Carolina.